Original title:
The Deep Sea's Embrace

Copyright © 2025 Creative Arts Management OÜ
All rights reserved.

Author: Sophia Kingsley
ISBN HARDBACK: 978-1-80587-376-1
ISBN PAPERBACK: 978-1-80587-846-9

Sanctuary of Serene Depths

In bubbles of laughter, fish do dance,
A clownfish slips in a goofy prance.
Octopus wrangles, a noodle of arms,
Tickling the corals with all of its charms.

Starfish are lounging, no need to rush,
While turtles are plotting a sly little hush.
The seaweed wiggles, it's quite a sight,
As jellyfish float in the soft moonlight.

Twilight in the Ocean's Hold

Kraken's got jokes, but nobody hears,
His eight-armed antics bring giggles and cheers.
A dolphin's choir sings off-key delight,
While seahorses tango under starlit night.

The pufferfish bubbles, grows round with glee,
While clam-shells snap in a snappy spree.
Anemones wave, they just want to play,
While turtles shout "Shell-abration!" all day!

Emptiness in the Currents

An empty old treasure chest makes a home,
For a crab who's decided it's time to roam.
He peeks out, then retreats, all sneaky and sly,
Avoiding the prying gaze of a passing fish eye.

A narwhal is dreaming of unicorn fame,
While eels play charades in a slippery game.
The fish try to gossip, it's quite the affair,
But end up just swimming in circles of air.

Cradle of the Sea

In a cradle of laughter, the sea creatures play,
A walrus is honing his stand-up display.
While plankton giggle with tiny little shimmies,
The sea cucumbers join in with their whimsies.

Seahorses shuffle to a jazzy old tune,
Bouncing along like balloons at a moon.
With bubbles and gurgles, the ocean's a blast,
In this watery wonder, we'll have a grand cast.

Secrets of the Currents

Bubbles rise, fish swim by,
Pink octopus wears a tie.
Seahorses dance, all in a row,
While jellyfish put on a show.

Sandy floors, crabs do the cha-cha,
Shells clapping like a grand ol' gala.
Starfish wink, what a delight,
In this underwater disco night.

Veil of Aquatic Shadows

Glow-in-the-dark squids give a fright,
Chasing shadows, oh what a sight!
A clownfish jokes, with a big red nose,
Tickling turtles, look how it goes.

Anglerfish shows off its great light,
But its jokes don't shine quite right.
Coral giggles and sways to the tune,
In this deep space where bubbles balloon.

Lullabies from the Blue Depths

Whale songs echo, softly they hum,
While clams join in, they go 'thump-thump!'
Dolphins leap, making waves in cheer,
Splashing the octopus, who peers near.

Turtle snores under a seaweed sheet,
While crabs sneak snacks, oh what a treat!
Feather stars twirl, joining the fun,
In the soft blue where sleep's begun.

The Siren's Call

Mermaids giggle, play hide and seek,
With fishy friends, they laugh and squeak.
A sea cucumber rolls in the sand,
While seahorse twins form a band.

Dancing barnacles sing silly tunes,
To the rhythm of sun and moon.
As waves gently rock, the laughter flows,
In this world where anything goes!

Mysteries of the Deep Waters

What swims below that swishy fin?
A crab with shades, counting his kin.
He sips on kelp, thinks he's so cool,
Debating fish laws, he makes his own rule.

The octopus juggles shells with glee,
While dolphins giggle, just waiting for tea.
A snail on the run in slow-motion chase,
Says, 'I'll win this race, just give me some space!'

Whispers from the Deep

Whispers echo through the briny blue,
"Hey there, fish, do you feel this too?"
A clownfish chuckles, "Not a joke, mate!
Speaking in bubbles, we can't be late!"

A sea turtle mumbles, "Did you hear that?
It's just a whale fart, imagine the spat!"
With coral as pillows, they nod and agree,
In the ocean's gossip, there's humor like free!

Beneath Velvet Waves

Beneath soft waves where laughter arises,
A shrimp wears a tie, he cleans up surprises.
He dances and twirls, a real party star,
Says, "Tell me your secret, I'll take you far!"

A pufferfish sighs, "No stress, just fluff!"
"I just blow up, ain't that enough?"
But the clownfish grins, "No worries, dear friend,
Life's just a joke that we all can pretend!"

Heart of the Ocean's Night

In the heart of the night, when creatures take flight,
A glowworm disco shines so bright.
Starfish in hats groove to the beat,
While jellyfish wiggle their glowing feet.

A sea slug sings, "Just don't bring the light,
I'm shy in my colors, but I'm quite the sight!"
Mollusks tapping rhythm, they all find their way,
In a whimsical world that won't let them sway!

Luminous Waters

In the depths where glowfish play,
And jellybeans float on display,
A crab wore a hat, quite askew,
He danced in the light, just for you.

Octopuses play peek-a-boo,
With squishy friends in shades of blue,
The seaweed swayed, fast and slow,
As fish told jokes, to row and row.

Journey to the Ocean's Heart

A turtle in shades of neon bright,
Chased after a starfish, what a sight!
They shared a laugh at a clam's bad pun,
While a whale joined in, just for fun.

A dolphin spun, with a flip and a twist,
Said, "Surfing's great, don't get me missed!"
The seagulls cawed, with a call so grand,
As they all agreed, 'We're in demand!'

Wave's Gentle Cradle

In a wrap of bubbles, the fish took a nap,
While a clam played music, a jazzy mishap,
Starfish played cards, with glee and delight,
As they bet all their shells, on a game late at night.

The waves rolled in with a splish and a splash,
As crabs in tuxedos made a grand dash,
They danced on the shore with a flip and a twirl,
Oh, to be part of their undersea whirl!

Oceanic Serenity

With a wink and a nod, the narwhals conspire,
To start an ocean circus, oh what a fire!
The plankton applauded from shimmering seats,
As the sea horse juggled, all wiggly beats.

A fish in a bowtie was telling tall tales,
While the gulls all laughed, flapping their sails,
The sea invited all, in its gleeful way,
To a party beneath, where all creatures play.

The Ocean's Eternal Song

Bubbles rise, fish giggle, a clown
Jellyfish dance like they own the crown.
Whales sing tunes, quite off-key,
Crabs tap dance, their own jamboree.

Mermaids snack on sushi rolls,
While octopuses play hide-and-seek goals.
Starfish sunbathe, yeah, they're quite bold,
Seahorses wear shades, if truth be told.

Turtles race with a seaweed twist,
Each lap taken, much too brisk.
Dolphins jump, making a splashy fuss,
Even the seaweed's got a fun bus.

In the depths, ocean humor flows,
Coral reefs chuckle, everybody knows.
So dive in deep for a whimsical reel,
Underwater laughter becomes so surreal!

Shadows of the Deep Blue Sea

Shadows wiggle, a sardine parade,
Just don't ask why they're all so afraid.
Lobsters waltz with a mischief grin,
While sea cucumbers just slowly spin.

Sharks wear glasses, oh what a sight,
Taking selfies with fish, feeling just right.
Eels tell jokes that make the sea laugh,
While barnacles sell seaweed on behalf.

Puffers puff, getting round and jolly,
Gentle giants are just so folly.
Plankton join in a giggly spree,
Inviting squid for a grand tea party.

Dancing shrimp leap with a cheery flair,
A crab starts a conga, quite unaware.
In the shadows, smiles never flee,
Life's a quirk in the deep blue spree!

Caressing the Underwater Silence

Silence hums, soft bubbles play,
A hermit crab sings, "Come join my stay!"
The seaweed sways with a playful cheer,
As fish throw a banquet—come grab a beer!

Anemones wiggle, tickle the fish,
While seahorses dream of their grandest wish.
Nudibranchs laugh, colors so bright,
Making snapshots, capturing light.

Giant clams gossip, sharing their tales,
While pair of dolphins sail gentle gales.
Each wave a joke, every splash a tease,
Life's a comedy, put your mind at ease.

So dive beneath where the fun's alive,
Join the party, take a deep dive.
With each sweet giggle from creatures so grand,
Underwater, the humor is truly unplanned!

Embraced by the Tides

Oh fish in tuxedos, dancing so neat,
They twirl and they swirl on their finned little feet.
With jellyfish jellies, a party so bright,
They wiggle and giggle, what a silly sight.

The crab in the corner, a pinch and a poke,
Tells jokes to the octopus, made from old smoke.
While seaweed sways to the rhythm so grand,
All creatures unite, it's a fun, funky band.

Depths Beyond the Light

In waters where sunlight rarely appears,
A dolphin plays tag, he's full of good cheer.
With bubbles and giggles, they dart and they dash,
Avoiding the angler, who waits for a flash.

A clownfish is grinning, his colors so loud,
He throws a big party, inviting the crowd.
With sea cucumbers grooving, the fun never ends,
Who knew ocean critters could be such good friends?

Beneath the Surface

A turtle in shades, cruising with style,
Says, "Slow and steady, I'll go the extra mile!"
The seaweed waves back, pretending to cheer,
While crabs tap dance round, raising a loud cheer.

A pufferfish pops, then he winks with a grin,
"Who needs a balloon? I can do that with skin!"
The sunken ship holds treasures, but what could they be?
"Just lost socks and old keys," says the fish with glee.

Fathoms of Forgotten Tales

A mermaid serenades, her voice like a song,
But sea bass just laugh, thinking she's gone wrong.
They jest and they jive, in the water they play,
Swapping tall tales at the end of the day.

An eel does a shimmy, the clownfish claps loud,
As starfish start twirling, they're drawing a crowd.
The bubble-blowing walrus, with a wink of his eye,
Turns every fish tale into a wild, wacky lie.

Dreams in the Deep

In an ocean of jelly, I went for a dive,
But a clam gave a wink, said, 'I'm quite alive!'
Seahorses giggled, all wearing their ties,
While sushi danced circles, oh what a surprise!

A fish wearing glasses gave wisdom to seek,
'Why chase the tide when you can just sneak?'
With bubbles for laughter, the dolphins did cheer,
'Join our underwater disco, bring your best beer!'

Crabs in tuxedos served shrimp on a plate,
The octopus DJ proclaimed, 'A fine date!'
Starfish flipped pancakes with syrupy glee,
And we all sang together, 'Under the sea!'

So if you're feeling blue and need some delight,
Remember the laughter that bubbles up bright.
For in this great ocean, where silliness swells,
Comes a treasure of joy that no one can sell!

Chasing the Abyssal Light

In the depths of the ocean, I wanted to shine,
But a squid made a face, said, 'You're crossing the line!'
With flashlights of laughter, we wandered around,
Turning shadows to giggles, oh what a sound!

A crab with a top hat declared, 'I can dance!'
As we twirled like mermaids, beached in a trance.
The eels turned to jellies, shook off their old fears,
While we toasted our friendship with bubble-filled cheers!

Dancing with turtles who had no sense of time,
We sang silly jingles, and it felt like a crime.
The anglerfish giggled, with its quirky bright lure,
Confetti from seaweed made this bash feel pure!

So if you're in search of an abyssal delight,
Just remember the fun that can glow in the night.
For beneath every wave, lies a dance and a laugh,
In the watery wonderlands, let's have a blast!

Reflections from the Dark Waters

In murky old waters where shadows reside,
I spotted a fish who was trying to hide.
With mirrors all around, it couldn't escape,
Looking like dinner all dressed up as a cape!

A shrimp with a problem, said, 'Life is a drag!'
'Til a starfish chimed in, 'Don't be a nag!'
With laughter and glee, they made quite the team,
Turning water to bubbles, fulfilling a dream!

The octopus pranced, sporting multiple shoes,
While crabs on the sidelines were trying to snooze.
'Why take life so seriously?' one seaweed crone quipped,
As she tossed out confetti that perfectly dripped!

So if you dive down where the dark waters flow,
Don't fear the reflections that come with the show.
For in the deep depths, there's joy to unwrap,
With every wave's chuckle, and every gurgled clap!

Beneath the Glistening Surface

Beneath waves that shimmer, all playful and bright,
A flounder called out, 'I'm a master of fright!'
At every turn tickled by bubbles and fun,
Where the fish told their jokes and the laughter would run!

A dolphin with chimes made a catchy new beat,
While the clam was a rapper, rapping fresh meat.
With each silly splash, the sea stars gave cheer,
And the seaweed ruled over those who held dear!

Mollusks wore crowns made from shells all around,
While the coral played games on a colorful mound.
Sip fish were beeping on sound systems loud,
As the waves threw a party that felt like a crowd!

So come on down where the glistening plays,
Where every fish knows all the silliest ways.
For beneath all the splendor, there's joy to explore,
In the depths of the ocean, you'll laugh evermore!

Reveries in Coral Kingdoms

In coral castles, fish do play,
With seaweed hats, they dance all day.
A crab tried salsa, stepped on a snail,
The ocean chuckled, what a tale!

Jellyfish wobble like they're on a spree,
Sipping on kelp with a side of sea.
Octopuses juggle with all of their arms,
While turtles nap, oblivious to charms!

Seahorses gossip about the waves,
Plotting a party in shimmering caves.
A clam whispered secrets, oh what a fuss,
As dolphins laughed, "That's fabulous!"

Underwater laughter echoes wide,
As fish ride the currents, full of pride.
The sea's a stage, it's simply divine,
With creatures who frolic, sip brine with wine!

Embrace of the Ocean's Heart

A whale tells jokes with a bass drum's beat,
As playful seals jump, swift on their feet.
Starfish play poker, with shells stacked neat,
While shrimp wear tuxedos, looking quite sweet.

A pufferfish blew up, thought it was grand,
Said, "Look at me! I'm the best in the band!"
Anemones giggle at all of the fuss,
While fish think, "Seriously, is that a plus?"

Coral reefs rock out, under moonlit spark,
With squids holding mics, singing well past dark.
The tide rolls in, with a soft, silly grin,
As crabs scratch their heads, "Where do we begin?"

The ocean's a dance floor, so full of cheer,
With jellybeans floating, oh what a sphere!
In this watery world, laughter is key,
As everyone bubbles with gleeful esprit!

Depths of Liquid Midnight

In the depths where the dark things drift,
   Glow worms party, giving a gift.
A fish claimed, "I glow, I steal the show,"
   While shy anglerfish flickered below.

Squids ink their way through midnight's dance,
   With krill spinning wildly, in a trance.
Cuttlefish change hues, a fabulous sight,
   As they blend in and out, full of delight.

At the bottom, a clam set up a bar,
   Mixing cocktail bubbles, oh how bizarre!
With sirens that sing, it's a wild affair,
   As sea cucumbers sway without a care!

In this fabulous gloom, where life's hearts beat,
   Every twist and turn is a laugh so sweet.
The ocean is bold, with humor and light,
   A joyride, oh what a deluge of sight!

Guardians of the Abyss

In shadows dwell creatures gleaming bright,
Guardians chuckling in the depths of night.
A snail's on patrol, but moves very slow,
While eels give high-fives, putting on a show.

A crab with a sword, feels like a knight,
Proclaims, "I protect this oceanic plight!"
With barnacles cheering on clammy thrones,
The octopus laughs as it tosses its bones.

The sea floor's a realm of quirky delight,
From lazy sea urchins to fish that ignite.
With laughter that bubbles like soft waves ashore,
Each guardian smiles, always wanting more!

As night falls softly, they gather around,
Exchanging their tales, how joy knows no bounds.
In this deep, dark abyss, it's never too grim,
For laughter and friendship reign ever so dim!

Dancers of the Deep

With twirls and swirls, the fish do glide,
They wear their scales like gowns of pride.
A crab tries to join, but oh so clunky,
Dancing with friends makes him feel funky.

A turtle joins in, slow but sincere,
Rolling those flippers, spreading good cheer.
The seaweed sways to the rhythmic beat,
While the octopus serves up snacks you can eat.

The jellyfish jive, glimmering bright,
Flashy and floaty, it's quite the sight.
They'll dance 'til the waves bring the day to an end,
While sea urchins giggle, it's quite the trend.

A whale joins the fun with a flip and a splash,
Creating a wave, oh what a crash!
The creatures of blue in a wild ballet,
In the underwater ball, they're here to stay!

The Caress of the Blue

The otter floats by, with a bubblegum grin,
His friend the dolphin joins in with a spin.
They play tag with a seagull above,
Singing sweet songs that echo with love.

A clam snaps shut, trying to join the fun,
But all he can do is hide in the sun.
While starfish watch, contemplating their fate,
Wondering if dance is worth the wait.

The sea cucumbers wiggle, oh what a sight,
They don't seem to care, feeling quite light.
They shimmy and shake, with a slosh and sway,
Thinking, why can't every day be playday?

With every splash, and every giggle,
The sea comes alive with a joyful wiggle.
Bubbles rise up like laughter afloat,
In the caress of the blue, they merrily gloat.

Legends of the Ocean Realm

In the depths of the blue, fish tell their tales,
Of mishaps with nets and adventures in gales.
A swordfish roars about battles he's fought,
While a shy little shrimp hides, feeling distraught.

The anglerfish grins, glowing and sly,
"I once played a trick on a curious guy!"
He baited a hook with his shimmering light,
And laughed to see fishermen take off in fright.

A wise old turtle drops wisdom so grand,
"Find joy in the waves and a friend's helping hand."
While the schools of the minnows all giggle and squawk,
As the octopus draws graffiti on rock.

The ocean's legends, so silly yet bold,
Turn deep blue drama into stories retold.
With laughter as currents, and joy as their theme,
The ocean is certainly not what it seems!

Reflections of the Infinite Blue

In the depths, reflections dance on the floor,
A catfish rolls by, looking to score.
He's wearing a crown made of shiny sea glass,
While a silly seahorse boggles with sass.

Anemones giggle, tickling the toes,
As fish dart around in bright, silly throes.
Clownfish make faces, all puffy and round,
While the waves take care of the playful sound.

The starfish is busy, striking a pose,
While the hermit crab swaps shells with his bros.
Every creature knows, under the sun's hue,
It's all about laughter in the infinite blue.

Then up from the surface, a splash and a cheer,
Seagulls overhead join the fun, oh dear!
With reflections of joy and a splashy delight,
The deep holds its secrets, and laughs through the night!

Solace in Aquatic Depths

In the ocean's vast ballet, fish dance with glee,
A crab plays the fiddle, just wait and see.
Octopuses juggle with style and flair,
While sea turtles snooze without a care.

A starfish complains of a ticklish drift,
As dolphins play games, giving fish a lift.
Coral reefs giggle, bright colors abound,
In this underwater circus, joy's always found.

Anglerfish glow like disco balls bright,
While sea cucumbers chill in the night.
A shark cracks a joke, in toothy delight,
Together they party, till morning's first light.

So if you feel blue or need a good laugh,
Dive into the waves, take a watery bath.
For life down below might be quite a sight,
Where laughter and bubbles fill up the night.

Entwined with the Ocean

A walrus wears sunglasses, and what a sight,
He's catching some rays, feeling just right.
Fish flip and flop, like they're in a race,
Each splash is a giggle, an underwater chase.

Seahorses shuffle in their quirky parade,
While jellyfish float like they're overplayed.
A clam tells a joke, but no one can hear,
As laughter erupts, echoing near.

Bubbles pop loudly, a fizzy ballet,
As the ocean's inhabitants frolic away.
With each little wave, the fun never ends,
In this watery realm, where all are good friends.

So grab your snorkel, come join the fun,
Under the waves, with laughter we run.
For life's more delightful in the ocean's delight,
Where humor runs deep, with morning till night.

Whispers of the Nautilus

In the depths of the ocean, a nautilus sways,
Whispering secrets of long-lost days.
He tells tales of sunken ships and gold,
While fish roll their eyes, they've heard it all told.

A rogue wave giggles, splashing with flair,
Tickling the fins of fish swimming there.
A clownfish in stripes, with jokes on the side,
Makes everyone chuckle on this vibrant ride.

The angelfish spin, like ballerinas aglow,
While a stingray steals kisses from below.
"Why did the crab never share his meal?"
"Because he was shellfish!" Oh, laugh, it's a steal!

With whispers and chuckles, the ocean composes,
A symphony of joy from its beautiful poses.
Diving with laughter, it's hard not to grin,
In waters filled with joy, where the fun will begin.

Melodies of Forgotten Tides

Down in the deep, there's a band made of shells,
They play underwater, with echoes and yells.
An eel plays the lute, a crab on the drums,
While bubbles burst forth with giggles and hums.

A planktonic party, it's really quite lit,
With phosphorescent lights, everything's a hit.
The tuna dance close, to the rhythm they sway,
In the water's warm groove, they just can't stay away.

A pufferfish pouts, but the crowd gives a cheer,
As a seaweed singer croons sweet tunes to the seer.
The waves tap their toes, in a grand ocean show,
Where laughter and melodies freely flow.

So dive down below, take a swim in delight,
Join the aquatic festivals, laugh through the night.
For within the great depths, the joy's never shoddy,
In the rapture of waves, join the frolicsome party!

The Allure of Mysterious Depths

In the ocean where fish wear hats,
A whale snorts bubbles, oh how it chats!
Octopuses dance with flair and style,
Crabs creep around with a humorous smile.

Giant squids play peek-a-boo, it's true,
With googly eyes in shades of blue.
They tickle the turtles, who giggle with glee,
While jellyfish float, looking fancy and free.

Fish throw parties, oh what a sight,
With snacks of seaweed, a pure delight!
They boogie and jiggle, creating a scene,
In this underwater world, laughter is queen.

So come take a plunge, dive and explore,
Where silliness reigns in the oceanic floor.
Embrace the quirks of life undersea,
In the depths of the ocean, let's all just be!

A Song of Sorrowful Seas

The fish all frown in a deep, blue space,
With seaweed hats that just don't fit their face.
Starfish see sad little crabs walk by,
And whisper to clams, 'Oh why, oh why?'

A dolphin sings a gloomy little tune,
While sharks in tuxedos sulk under the moon.
The seahorses sigh, as if to tease,
The world is a mess with these sorrowful seas.

The mermaids cry, their scales turning gray,
For they lost their bling in a clam buffet.
"Where's our treasure?" they pout with disdain,
As fish seek out laughter to hide their pain.

But wait—what's this? A joke just got told!
The octopuses chuckle, their humor bold.
So join in the laughter, join in the fun,
And dance through the waves—underneath the sun!

Glimpses of Undersea Realms

Bright colored corals with wiggly tails,
Invite the fish for their silly trails.
Nemo plays tag with a silly old crab,
While squids shoot ink, oh what a drab!

Turtles take snapchats, looking quite cool,
With filters of bubbles, they rule the school.
Dolphins do flips, making quite the scene,
While sea cucumbers just lounge in between.

The anglerfish glows with a charming grin,
'Come closer, dear fish, let the fun begin!'
But watch out for clowns, not the funny type,
These fishy jesters can give quite a fright!

In this realm where laughter dances about,
Adventure awaits, without a doubt.
So dive into dreams, let the waters swirl,
Where giggles and joy make the ocean twirl!

In the Heart of the Abyss

In the darkest depths, a hippo floats by,
Trying to tango with an octopus shy.
They twirl and they swirl, causing quite a fuss,
While mermaids giggle, saying, 'Look at us!'

The angler's light is a disco ball,
Where sea urchins gather for the grand hall.
The fish in bow ties grimace and grin,
Dancing with seaweed, let the fun begin!

Anemones sway with a jellyfish beat,
As grumpy old sharks just can't take the heat.
They ponder their lives in this silly soiree,
Wishing for snacks, a delightful buffet.

But laughter erupts in the depths of the night,
With bubbles and banter, it all feels so right.
Embrace the abyss, where humor's set free,
In the heart of the ocean, just let it be!

Murmurs of the Tide

A crab in a tux, doing the cha-cha,
Swirling with fish in a water fiesta.
The octopus juggles, oh what a sight,
While dolphins dance in the moon's silver light.

A whale tells a joke, but it's hard to hear,
With bubbles and splashes, it's tough like a spear.
The starfish giggles, it tickles its toes,
While the clam munches popcorn, oh, how it glows!

A seahorse rides waves just like a cool dude,
With shades on its eyes, it's quite in the mood.
The plankton hold parties, they shimmer and sway,
In the ocean's vast hall, they dance night and day.

So come join the fun, leave worries behind,
In the splash of the tide, pure joy you will find.
With laughter and bubbles, we'll sing with glee,
In this wacky water world, come swim with me!

Enchantment of the Hidden Depths

A fish with a wig sings karaoke,
While a turtle plays tambourine, oh pokey!
The anglerfish shines, it's quite the dazzling tease,
As seagulls applaud from their posts in the breeze.

The jellyfish float, all dressed in their best,
With ribbons and bows, they dance with great zest.
A lobster's on stage, cracking jokes to the crowd,
With crustacean charm, he makes everyone loud!

Coral reefs party with colors so bright,
Blowing bubbles while twirling, what pure delight!
They invite every creature, from big to the small,
In this underwater rave, there's fun for us all.

So swim through this magic, where laughter is king,
In the depths of the sea, let's dance and let's sing.
With merriment flowing like currents so bold,
Join the splashy jamboree, embrace the uncontrolled!

Secrets of the Sea Serpent

A sea serpent grins, with a wink and a twirl,
It's spinning like tops, giving a whirl.
It dips and it dives, with gleeful intent,
Stealing kelp hats; oh, what a fun prank!

A clam with a mustache jokes with a wink,
While fish in tuxedos try not to sink.
The octopus cheers, it's quite the debacle,
As the mermaids giggle at every odd angle.

The serpent decides to throw quite a bash,
With games and with snacks, oh, what a splash!
Bubbles and laughter fill every nook,
As critters sneak treats from the cool ocean cook.

So if you should wander where secrets abound,
Join the serpent's party, where joy knows no bound.
In waters of giggles, where fun takes the lead,
Every sea-dweller revels in laughter and speed!

Shadows in the Marine Twilight

Under waves where the shadows start to sway,
Creatures gather around for a nightly play.
A dolphin with glasses reads tales of the sea,
While a crab acts the hero, oh, who could it be?

The midnight is rich with giggles and sound,
A shrimp plays the spoons; it's the talk of the ground.
The flounder flips cards, letting luck take its flight,
While jellybeans glow in the soft, gentle light.

Stars twinkle above like bubbles on cue,
As the sea creatures gather, here's what they do:
They dance and they tumble, they cavort and glide,
While mermaids critique their best-twirling vibe!

So join in the fun, let the waters embrace,
In the shadows where smiles paint each happy face.
With whimsy and wonder where night comes alive,
Let's celebrate laughter, together we thrive!

Beneath the Veil of Stars

In the depths where fish wear shades,
A jellyfish twirls like it's making parades.
A crab doing ballet, with moves so spry,
While octopus painters create art on the fly.

A whale sings jokes that tickle the eels,
And turtles exchange their best meal deals.
The seaweed sways, it's having a ball,
With dolphins dancing, they invite us all.

Fish gossip and giggle, they splash in delight,
Fins flapping freely, oh what a sight!
A sea cucumber slips, tries to impress,
But all that it does is cause quite a mess.

So join in the fun, take a dive today,
Where laughter and bubbles lead the way.
From the waves to the depths, let humor reign,
In this watery world, joy is the main gain.

Mysteries of the Waters' Embrace

Beneath the waves, a treasure of laughs,
A clam that can't close, making silly gaffes.
Starfish play poker, with shells as their stakes,
While sea urchins joke about what it takes.

A pufferfish giggles, swelling with pride,
As a grouper grins wide, like it just won a ride.
Mermaids with humor, they tell ocean tales,
While squids throw confetti from their slimy sails.

Anemones tickle with tentacles bright,
As a sea lion leaps, oh what a sight!
Fish on a mission to spread joy around,
In this watery world, pure silliness is found.

So dive into the laughter, don't miss the fun,
In the mysteries below, we're all number one!
With gags aplenty, the sea is the place,
To giggle and splash in this grand ocean space.

Songs of the Submerged

Under the waves, a quirky choir,
Sardines sing songs that never tire.
A conch shell comically shouts out a tune,
While clownfish laugh beneath the pale moon.

Goby fish strut, with flair and with grace,
An anglerfish grins, lighting up its face.
The chorus of bubbles adds a silly beat,
As fish do the cha-cha, with wiggly feet.

A sea horse twirls in a tiny ballet,
While krill share gossip as they glide and sway.
In this ocean concert, the fun takes a dive,
Where the music of laughter keeps everyone alive.

So cheer for the bubbles and sing to the tide,
Join the aquatic parade, take it in stride.
For the undersea songs are a joyous surprise,
With humor and fun that forever can rise.

Echoes from the Ocean Floor

Down in the deep, where the silliness swells,
A fish tells a joke, and the sea anemone yells.
"Why did the crab never share its snack?
Because it was shellfish," oh what a quack!

A clam's got a secret, it can't keep it sealed,
While flounders play hide-and-seek, oh what a field!
Whales make up riddles, trying to soar,
As the bubbles around them rise, evermore.

The sea cucumber's late, it's stuck in the sand,
Its friends all giggle, they just can't stand.
The sea stars roll, with laughter so bright,
In the echoes of waves, all is pure delight.

So dive in and listen, let the giggles unfold,
With tales from the depths, as the stories are told.
For beneath the surface, where joy has no bound,
Laughter and music forever resound.

Underwater Serenade

Fish in tuxedos dance with glee,
Jellyfish join the wild jamboree.
Crabs wear crowns, ooh what a sight,
Bubbles burst, bringing pure delight.

Octopus strums on a coral guitar,
Playing tunes that travel far.
Seahorses spin, like a disco ball,
While clams chuckle—best party of all!

Starfish twist in a limbo line,
Eels slither, making it divine.
But a whale bursts through with a happy song,
Bringing all the fish along!

In a realm where laughter swims,
Every bubble's laughter brims.
Let's dance and twirl, enjoy the show,
Underwater, where joy will flow!

The Language of the Waves

Waves speak riddles, what do they say?
"Surfboards make a great lunch tray!"
Seagulls giggle, "Is that a fish?"
"Or just your soggy sandwich wish?"

Turtles wear glasses, reading the tides,
"Dear Dolphins, let's play—no need to hide!"
They play charades, a splash and a shout,
Who knew the ocean could twist about?

Crabs conspire, "Let's start a band!
With shells for drums, how grand, how grand!"
Underwater, they jam through the night,
Playing tunes with joy and delight.

The waves just laugh, their secrets they keep,
As the sea creatures waltz and leap.
Join this dance, let your heart be brave,
In the rhythm, find a wave!

Abyssal Whispers

In the depths, where shadows play,
Creatures gossip in a quirky way.
A clam says, "Can you hear that sound?
It's just a whale on the prowling round!"

A squid starts plotting with style and flair,
"Let's start a rumor, the crabs should beware!"
With colorful ink, they scribble and scrawl,
Secrets swim deep in this watery hall.

A pufferfish puffs in playful jest,
"Who can out-swim the octopus' best?"
Everyone giggles, and the sharks grin wide,
While mermaids join in the laughter tide.

So deep down below, where jokes take their seat,
The depths are alive with laughter so sweet.
Abyssal whispers carry with glee,
In this underworld party, come join and see!

Touched by the Ocean's Breath

Waves roll in, with a tickle and tease,
Seagulls squawk, soaring with ease.
They dive for snacks, oh what a sight,
As the tides giggle with sheer delight.

A sandy crab with a sunhat tall,
Rolls on the beach, he's having a ball.
"Do the wave!" he shouts to a pal,
With a flip-flop splash, oh what a gal!

Saltwater tickles as the fish take flight,
Splashing around in the soft moonlight.
"Catch me if you can!" a playful trout sings,
While the dolphins leap like they have wings.

As the sun sets low, it's time to jest,
The ocean holds secrets, but here's the best—
With every wave and every breath,
Laughter lingers, defying death!

Kisses of the Tidal Wave

A wave comes in with a cheeky grin,
Slapping the shore, it's a playful sin.
"Catch me if you can!" it seems to say,
As seagulls cackle and dive in play.

Flip-flops fly like kites in the breeze,
While hapless beachgoers trip with ease.
Sandcastles crumble, swept by the spree,
Those tidal kisses, so wild and free.

Oh, frothy friend of the sunlit day,
With laughter and splashes, you dance and sway.
The surfboard's now a surf-sled on land,
Scooting along like it's part of the band.

With swimsuits tangled, all in a whirl,
You steal our hearts, you mischievous pearl.
Every curve and splash is a giggly chance,
To dive and dip in your ocean dance.

The Ocean's Lullaby

Beneath the waves, a sleepy hum,
Fish serenade with their gurgling drum.
A crab taps out a funky beat,
While turtles sway, oh so discreet.

Jellyfish twirl in a fluorescent show,
Winking at starfishes, putting on a glow.
Seahorses dance, they're quite the sight,
In an underwater rave, they party all night.

Hermit crabs trade shells, it's a stylish affair,
While clams hide their pearls with delicate care.
An octopus juggles, with eight arms he sways,
In this quirky world, it's a wacky ballet.

So drift away on this bubbly spree,
With laughter and bubbles, float wild and free.
The ocean croons softly, a jokester supreme,
In this watery cradle, we all share a dream.

Journey to the Midnight Depths

In the depths where shadows prance,
Emerald fish start a midnight dance.
A dolphin jokes, swims up with glee,
"Where's the party? It's just you and me!"

Anglerfish flick their glowy bait,
But no one bites—they think it's fate.
"Join the conga line!" they cheep and chatter,
While eels do the twist, all think they're flatter.

The squid made ink, a shade of blue,
Wrote funny poems, yes, it's true.
But bubbles burst their secrets untold,
As the fish giggle loud, being bold.

With a wink from the stars on the surface above,
Creatures of night share some ocean love.
So dive in this laughter, with every fin flip,
In the midnight depths, take a giggly trip.

Threnody for the Forgotten Deep

Old shipwrecks hum with a ghostly tune,
While barnacles snack on a crusty moon.
Whales whisper secrets, ancient and deep,
About treasure chests in a fabled sleep.

The mermaids giggle, brushing their hair,
"Be careful," they sing, "if you even dare!"
With fishy scales and a wink of the eye,
They lure you close with a mischievous sigh.

Octopuses play cards; they're quite the team,
"A royal flush!" one claims, "or maybe a dream?"
While squids squirt ink like a messy bouquet,
In this underwater gala, we'll giggle away.

As seaweed sways with a top hat dance,
And rogue tides swirl in a merry prance.
Let's toast to the creatures we may not meet,
In the murky embrace, isn't life sweet?

Siren's Lullaby

In the coral lounge, fish line up bright,
A siren sings tunes, but they're a wee fright.
Seahorses dancing, they slip and they slide,
While octopuses giggle, they can't help but hide.

With bubbles of laughter, the dolphins partake,
A clam starts to snore, oh what a mistake!
Anemones sway, they tickle the squids,
Casting all worries like bubbles from lids.

The starfish debate who's the silliest star,
Each one claims a title, this isn't too far.
But the oyster pipes up, "I'm the real gem!
Just pearly and lovely, don't judge on a whim!"

As waves rock the boat, the laughter cascades,
Underwater giggles, the fun never fades.
Each scale and each fin, they dance through the night,
In this aquatic ball, it's a comical sight.

Shadows of the Blue

In the shadows they gather, the fish in a spree,
Laughing at bubbles that float from the sea.
A crab wears a top hat, a sight to behold,
He winks with his eyes, so smug and so bold.

A turtle on stilts thinks he's quite the pro,
But stumbles and tumbles, what a funny show!
The eels play charades, with quite the flair,
To guess the odd dance, you'd need curls in your hair.

A jellyfish jives, with swirls and with grace,
While the seaweed sways, oh what a strange place!
The angles they take, like a twist of fate,
Are punctuated by laughter, it's never too late.

The anglerfish's light, a beacon of cheer,
Luring in laughter, come gather right here!
In the depths of the blue, where shadows take flight,
Whimsical wonders occur with delight.

Currents of Solitude

Deep down in the depths, where the quiet does dwell,
A fish flips a fin, as it says, "All is well!"
The squid writes a sonnet, in flowing ink streams,
While crabs throw confetti, in the land of their dreams.

But solitude's tricky, it plays out in jest,
A whale with a cold, now that's quite the fest!
He sneezes so loudly, it shakes up the floor,
And all of his buddies swim out, to explore.

Seashells have gossip, they whisper and chime,
About the lone fish, oh, it's party time!
The plankton all giggle, in clusters they hide,
As the ocean bursts forth, with mirth, just like tide.

In currents of laughter, the blue sea spins bright,
Each creature unique, bringing joy day and night.
In solitude's arms, together they'll grow,
With their quirky antics, the ocean's a show.

Tide's Tender Touch

As tides roll in, with a playful little nudge,
The sea slinks around, but does it judge?
Seashells are making the best of their time,
With beach balls of kelp, how silly and prime!

A dolphin's out surfing, on waves of delight,
Catching laughs as he jumps, what a glimmering sight!
Starfish spin like tops, all ready for fun,
While crabs hold a game night, all under the sun.

The seagulls dive down, they squawk and they play,
Playing peek-a-boo with the waves in dismay.
A clam hides his face, thinks he's such a pro,
But the tide's tender touch gives him quite the show!

As sunset approaches, they gather in cheer,
In this watery world, where laughter rings clear.
In the dance of the surf and the call of the sea,
The tides wrap around with their playful decree.

Aqua's Whisper

The fish wear hats, oh what a sight,
They swim in circles, day and night.
A crab plays chess with a lazy snail,
While jellyfish tell tales of a giant whale.

A turtle jogs with sneakers on,
Chasing bubbles till they're gone.
The octopus paints with colorful glee,
Creating murals beneath the sea.

A dolphin dances, oh so spry,
Making friends with a passing pie.
Seahorses gallop, what a race,
While a clownfish tries to find his place.

With laughter echoing in every wave,
The ocean's a stage, a funny rave.
Who knew the depths could be so fun?
Beneath the surface, silliness won!

Abyssal Caress

An anglerfish with a glowing grin,
Invites the other fish to join in.
They form a band, all scales and cheer,
Playing tunes that all can hear.

A starfish thinks it's a rock band star,
While a plankton floats, a tiny car.
With deep-sea jelly spreading sweet vibes,
The disco's on, complete with jibes.

The shrimp, they dance on shrimping boats,
In seas of laughter, sharing notes.
A whale makes jokes, it's quite absurd,
As all the fishes cheer and slurred.

In this kingdom of laughs and splashes,
Even the seaweed has funny flashes.
With every current and wave's embrace,
The ocean's a party, a joyous place!

Beneath the Waves

There's a clam that croons a happy tune,
While a seahorse twirls in a silver moon.
Crabs wear sunglasses to look so cool,
As fish join in for a silly school.

A manta ray glides like a smooth old dude,
While tiny shrimp prance, oh how they're glued.
With bubbles of laughter, they rise and fall,
In this underwater town, fun's for all.

A pufferfish blows up from sheer delight,
While a barnacle reads a book each night.
The sardines have a secret quest,
To find a treasure, in jest, not a test.

What wonders dwell, beneath the blue?
Where creatures share giggles, it's all true.
With each splash and dash, the fun won't pause,
In the depths of the sea, it deserves applause!

Echoes of the Ocean Floor

A lobster jokes about his fancy claws,
Saying he's ready for applause.
While a sea cucumber, snug in a bed,
Dreams of fish that dance on their head.

With bubbles floating, jokes swim near,
Kraken's ticklish, but have no fear.
A giant squid with a funny hat,
Trying to tickle a passing cat.

Down where the sun rays barely can peek,
A narwhal raps, it's quite unique.
Anemones sway, laughing all day,
As the tides bring silliness their way.

Echoes of laughter fill the salty air,
In this fun zone that's beyond compare.
With every laugh and every roar,
The ocean thrives with a jovial core!

Dance of the Bioluminescent

In darkness they twirl, a neon show,
Fish with disco moves, putting on a glow.
A jellyfish spins, with grace it sways,
While a crab attempts to join the ballet craze.

They flicker and flash, creating a scene,
An underwater party, in aqua sheen.
Clownfish are giggling, fish in tuxedos,
As they breakdance on corals, looking like heroes.

The seahorses waltz, with tails intertwined,
Bubbles are popping, the dance floor's refined.
Bass beats are thumping, from shells in the sand,
It's a party below where no-one had planned.

So if you dive down, with fins all a-swish,
Join in the fun, there's only one wish—
Dance with the fish on this colorful wave,
In the glow of the sea, we laugh and behave!

Tides of Forgotten Memories

As the tide rolls in, it whispers my name,
Telling old tales of a fishy fame.
A crab with a hat and a wise little stare,
Recalls a great battle with a pair of old chairs.

Starfish grumble, quite stuck on the floor,
They reminisce about trips to the shore.
An octopus claims he once had a date,
With a beautiful mermaid, now that's quite great!

But the memories fade, like sand through a sieve,
The fish just swim on, that's how they live.
Waved goodbyes to those old tales of glory,
Now they just giggle at their own silly story.

Yet here comes a surf, with a splash and a roar,
Washing away tales that they once bore.
With a flip and a twirl, they laugh and they cheer,
Celebrating now, for the future is here!

Beneath the Surface of Dreams

In the ocean of dreams, where fish wear their hats,
A swordfish is fencing with two clever spats.
A band of sea turtles, in glasses so round,
Are plotting a heist for lost treasure they found.

Lobsters play poker, with shells all a-glow,
While squids spin a yarn, putting on quite the show.
Mermaids are giggling, tails in a twist,
As the sand dollars gossip, plotting a tryst.

They whirl and they twirl, beneath bubble soft skies,
With laughter echoing, as time swiftly flies.
The sharks wear bow ties, looking dapper and neat,
As they host a ball with a funky sea beat.

But just like in dreams, morning comes with a rush,
The creatures disperse in a splashing, loud hush.
Yet they'll always remember those nights under streams,
Where fun and fish tales danced in silver beams!

A Cavern of Silence

In a cavern so quiet, where echoes are few,
A clam plays the harp, as soft as the dew.
A rockfish plays hide-and-seek all alone,
While sea cucumbers lounge, claiming the throne.

They whisper sweet secrets, too quiet for sound,
And giggle at bubbles that float all around.
The octopus watches, a trick up his sleeve,
As he wraps up the silence, it's hard to believe!

Anemones dance in a slow, graceful swirl,
While eels tell tall tales of their underwater whirl.
But the silence is broken by a loud turtle snore,
As the whole cavern shakes, from ceiling to floor.

They laugh at the noise, their peace sent astray,
But in this stillness, they still find a way.
To share in the joy, the chuckles, the cheer,
In a cavern of silence, where laughter draws near!

In the Arms of the Abyss

Bubbles rise like floating dreams,
Jellyfish dance in silly beams.
An octopus gave me a wink,
Said, 'Quit fussing, just have a drink!'

Fish wear ties, they swim in suits,
Gossiping clams in fancy boots.
A crab tried to steal my hat,
I told him, 'Dude, you're such a brat!'

Mermaids laugh with fins on show,
Pooling secrets, down below.
With seaweed snacks and shrimp cocktails,
They sing of ships and epic tales.

Sunlight flickers, a fish parade,
Whales serenade in grand parade.
But beware, the sea's a tease,
With ticklish tides and bubbly knees.

Currents of Enchantment

Seahorses riding waves of mirth,
Throwing parties for the sea's worth.
Sand dollars cracking jokes on sand,
While clumsy starfish try to stand.

Dolphins leap with acrobatic grace,
Doing somersaults in the briny space.
Anemones tickle passing fins,
A crab bets more than it ever wins.

Turtles gossip with a lazy yawn,
'Who gave you that shell? It looks so worn!'
Blowfish puffed up in jest,
Grinning wide, they know they're best.

But beware the jester, the shark in suit,
Telling fish tales that bear no root.
For in this realm of playful charm,
Laughter's the best nautical charm!

Undercurrents of Solitude

Beneath the waves, a quiet sigh,
Where plankton dream and seaweed lie.
A solo fish in a tranquil spree,
Hoping for company, just one buddy!

A pelican squawks, it's a bit too loud,
As waves wrap round in a silvery shroud.
I named my rock; it's named alone,
We share our thoughts in a whispered tone.

Solitude's a funny friend,
With sea currents, we pretend.
An air bubble joins the chat,
Floating by, says, 'What's up, cat?'

But tides pull in and out with glee,
Waves bounce back, setting my mind free.
Here in loneliness, I'm quite spry,
Just a fish and my rock, oh, my!

Nightfall in the Ocean's Grasp

In the moonlit waters, creatures peek,
While lanternfish play hide-and-seek.
An eel with glasses reads a map,
Finding the way to the perfect nap.

Crickets chirp on the ocean floor,
Celebrating night; oh, the tales they bore!
A shrimp with attitude, took center stage,
Claiming the night is all the rage.

Octopi in pajamas, so chic,
Tell tall tales about their streak.
Once, a fish swam right through my dream,
Wearing a crown, oh, what a scheme!

Yet as waves lull the world to sleep,
A turtle's snore is deep and steep.
In the embrace of darkened seas,
Life's a party; a ticklish tease!

Secrets in the Sapphire Depths

In the depths where the fish wear shoes,
They gossip and giggle, sharing bright hues.
A crab cracks jokes, with a pinch of flair,
While octopuses dance with a curious air.

The seaweed sways with a ticklish cheer,
As starfish laugh, 'We have no fear!'
Anemones sway, in their polka-dot gowns,
While the dolphin flips and the sea turtle frowns.

Pirates have treasure, but it's full of snacks,
With chocolate coins instead of gold hacks.
The mermaids sing songs to tickle your throat,
While seahorses race on a bubble-filled boat.

So dive in deep and join the fun,
Where fish tell tales, and the laughter's never done.
In sapphire realms where the silly roam free,
The ocean's secrets are waiting for thee!

The Embrace of Ocean's Shadows

In the shadows where jellyfish float,
They've opened a club with a glow-in-the-dark coat.
The clownfish tell jokes, while oysters just pout,
As the stingrays play games, there's no need to shout.

A turtle's slow dance brings giggles galore,
While sea cucumbers open their door.
The pufferfish pop with laughter, it seems,
As they share tales of their bubble-filled dreams.

The anglerfish flickers, a light on his head,
As he tells the freshest seafood bread.
The seaweed whispers secrets so sly,
Just don't mind the octopus rolling his eye.

So plunge into waters where laughter runs free,
In oceanic shadows, come find glee!
With fishy friends joining in on the spree,
Laughter and bubbles await under the sea!

Timelessness of the Abyss

In the abyss where time takes a nap,
The fish play charades, in a colorful trap.
A whale hums tunes of the olden days,
While plankton dance in their bioluminescent ways.

Ghostly ships drift by, with a creaky old crew,
Who tell silly stories of what they once knew.
The eels pull pranks, with a flick of their tails,
While deep-sea creatures share salty old tales.

A sponge jokes around, soaking up fun,
With a wink and a wiggle, he says he's done.
The coral reefs chuckle, the clownfish in line,
In the timeless abyss, all is simply divine!

So come take a dive, where the laughter won't cease,
In playful waters that dance with a peace.
With quirky sea creatures, it's no riddle,
In the depths of time, life's just like a fiddle!

Chronicles of the Silent Ocean

In the silent ocean, where whispers arise,
Fishes wear glasses, discussing the skies.
The sea urchins giggle, they poke and they prickle,
While a dolphin plays tunes, doing tricks like a pickle.

The squid tells a story, in colors so bright,
With tales of the shipwrecks lost to the night.
The hermit crab scuttles, his home on his back,
With a laugh and a wink, he follows the track.

Barnacles grumble, they're stuck to their spots,
As they cling to old boats, sharing fishy thoughts.
The deep-sea vents bubble, as if they could speak,
With stories and secrets, they play hide-and-seek.

So come swim with us, where the quiet sings loud,
In the chronicles of the ocean, we're all so proud.
With laughter and joy in every strange nook,
In the depths of the silence, come take a look!

Light in the Deep

Bright fish with silly grins,
Swimming in circles, like lazy twins.
Jellyfish glow like disco balls,
While octopus grooves and gently sprawls.

Crabs wear hats, all fancy and neat,
Strutting around on their little feet.
Eels play peek-a-boo behind the rocks,
Making jokes about swim trunks and socks.

A clam cracks jokes, his shell can't hold,
While starfish snicker, their laughter bold.
Underwater laughter, bubbling with glee,
Life's just a party, come join, don't flee!

Dance of the Sea Spirits.

Mermaids twirl in glittery fins,
Salsa dancing as the sea begins.
Seahorses trot in fancy attire,
While dolphins leap, their spirits on fire.

A crab with a wig takes center stage,
With a funky dance, he acts his age.
Seaweed sways like it's in a trance,
While sharks wait patiently for their chance.

Anemones wave, like they're in a play,
While clowns in the reef say, "Who wants to stay?"
Each wave brings giggles, a splash of delight,
Under the surface, the fun feels just right!

Whispers of Ocean Abyss

Bubbles rise up with secrets so sly,
A clam holds the mic, giving it a try.
"Why did the fish cross the road?" he muses,
"To get to the other tide, where it snoozes!"

Squid paint portraits with their ink so grand,
While seagrass shakes in a dance, so planned.
Pufferfish puffs up just to look cool,
But really he's shy; he's just playing the fool.

Grouper fish gossip, they're never quite hush,
While shrimp with their tunes have the ocean in a rush.
Echoes that ripple through waters of blue,
Tell tales of silliness, from a fish's point of view!

Echoes Beneath Sapphire Waves

Bubble-blowers making quite the sound,
With sea turtles spinning round and round.
Crabs in a conga, so sprightly and spry,
While pufferfish giggle as they float by.

Starfish tell tales of their land-bound friends,
Who dance on the shore, where the fun never ends.
Whales hum a tune that's cheeky and bright,
With dolphins chiming in, to everyone's delight.

Each splash carries laughter, a wave of pure cheer,
Where every quick dive brings giggles near.
Sapphire waves echo their glee all around,
In the depths of the ocean, joy can be found!